A Miracle
The Story of
Isa Ibn Maryam ﷺ

Hanifa Rahman

Illustrated by

Eman Salem

A Miracle – The Story of Isa ibn Maryam ﷺ

First Published in 2024 by
THE ISLAMIC FOUNDATION

Distributed by
KUBE PUBLISHING LTD
Tel +44 (0)1530 249230
E-mail: info@kubepublishing.com
Website: www.kubepublishing.com

Text copyright © Hanifa Rahman, 2024
Illustrations copyright © Eman Salem, 2024

All rights reserved.
No part of this publication may be reproduced,
stored in a retrieval system, or transmitted in any form or by any means,
electronic, mechanical, photocopying, recording or otherwise,
without the prior permission of the copyright owner

Author Hanifa Rahman
Illustrator Eman Salem
Art Direction Iman Anwar
Book Design Nasir Cadir

A Cataloguing-in-Publication Data record for this book is available
from the British Library

ISBN 978-0-86037-938-6
eISBN 978-0-86037-943-0

Printed by: Elma Basim Turkey

Contents

Hannah's Prayer	4
The Unusual Encounter	8
Birth of a Prophet	12
Baby Isa ﷺ	17
Isa ﷺ the Prophet	20
An Evil Scheme	24
The Ascension	26
References	32

Hannah's Prayer

This is the story of a miracle,

a miracle like no other.

In a quiet and deserted plain,

Maryam *'alayhas salaam* became a mother.

It all began in the holy land,

the land of Bayt al-Maqdis,

Where Imran resided with his wife;

content, although they were childless.

Hannah was the wife of Imran,

a most pious and noble lady.

She yearned to have a child and prayed,

"O Allah, please answer my prayer and bless me."

And so blessed she was with a baby,

untouched by Satan.

So pure and protected,

they named her… Maryam.

Maryam *'alayhas salaam*,
Allah chose her above all women.
Through her youth she remained virtuous;
inquisitive and intelligent.

The best of all women;
she is to be honoured and respected.
So focussed she was in worship;
neither feeling lazy, nor distracted.

Under the care of her uncle, Zakariyya,
Maryam did spend her days.
In the sacred mosque of al-Aqsa;
most devout and chaste in her ways.

For this she was rewarded with special sustenance,

a variety of luscious fruits.

Those of Winter she enjoyed in Summer;

whilst in Winter she found the Summer produce!

All this especially for Maryam

was sent down from the heavens.

They asked, "from where has all this appeared?"

She replied, "Allah gives to whomever He pleases."

The Unusual Encounter

Now, one day a strange thing happened

whilst Maryam was engaged in prayer.

A figure appeared before her;

it was Angel Jibra'eel with glad tidings to bear.

"I seek refuge in Allah,"

pious Maryam immediately proclaimed.

"Do not come near me,

for I have sought protection in Allah's Name."

He assured her, "Do not be frightened,

as I am God's Messenger,

you shall be blessed with a child," he said,

"A Prophet of Allah."

What a test this was for Maryam!

Now suddenly pregnant with a child.

Yet, she trusted in the plan of Allah,

and so patiently she endured this trial.

As the miracle grew inside of her,

they formed a very special bond.

Maryam wondered what was in store

for this baby, of whom she was so fond.

What special purpose will her baby serve?

What great challenges will he encounter?

Will his people believe in him and pay heed?

Or will they turn on him and make him suffer?

Not knowing, Maryam turned to Allah;

for in His provision and protection, she was sure.

Allah the Most Gracious, the Most Merciful

would guide and care for them, just as He had done before.

When the time came for the baby's arrival,

Maryam grew anxious and afraid.

Doubtful her people would understand,

she hoped for help, and so she prayed.

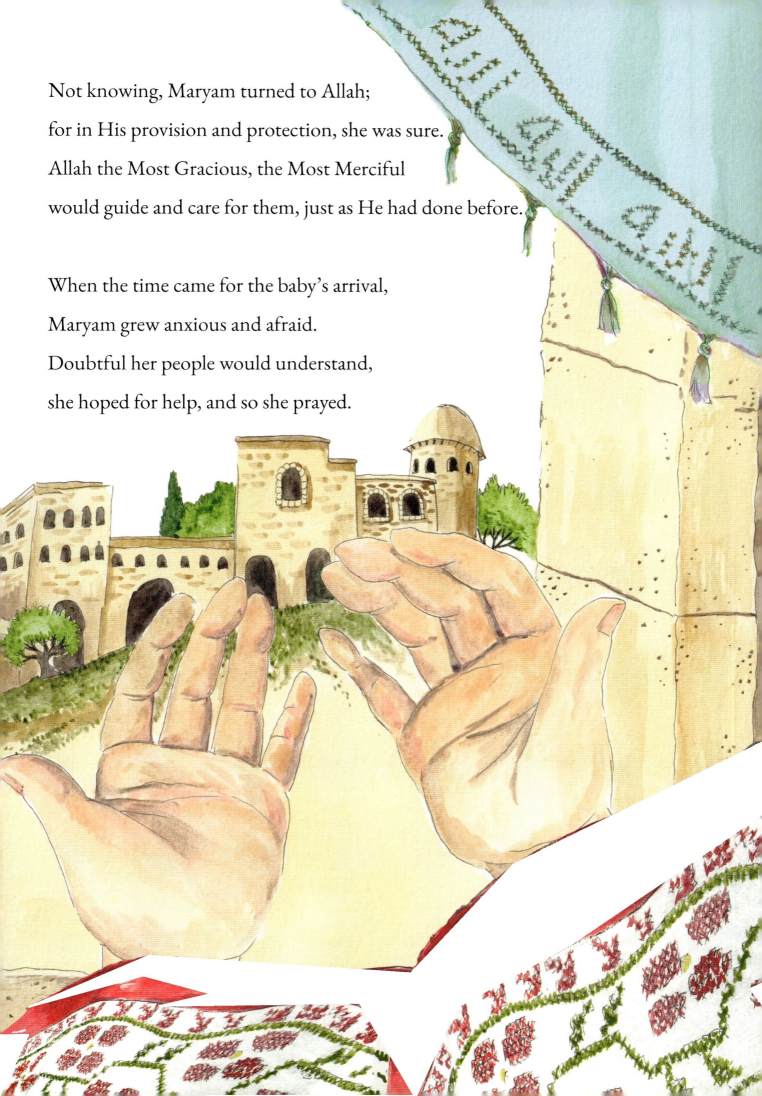

The Birth of a Prophet

As the throes of labour came upon her
and the pain became a burden;
dear Maryam, weak and in desperation,
wished she was a thing long forgotten.

But Allah was always watching over her
as was part of His Mighty plan;
to see who will persevere in times of hardship,
endure His trial and carry on.

And though seized by her distress,
Maryam remained resolute in her faith.
With trust in the Mercy of Allah
she believed she would be guided and safe.

All alone and in anguish,

Maryam retreated to a place far away.

There, she rested against a date-palm.

"*La tahzani*, do not worry", she heard a voice say.

"Allah has made a spring gush beneath you,

so quench your thirst.

Now shake the tree," the voice continued,

"and you shall find dates fall to the earth."

Subhan Allah! What comfort,

at a time of great distress!

For Maryam relied on Allah,

and it is in the remembrance of Him, that hearts find rest.

And so was born Prophet Isa ibn Maryam ﷺ;

born without a father.

A Prophet like Prophet Adam ﷺ;

a Miracle, a Messiah.

*Indeed, the example of Jesus to Allah is like that of Adam.
He created him from dust; then He said to him, "Be," and he was.*
(Quran 3: 59)

Baby Isa ﷺ

Baby Isa ﷺ was finally here;

a specially selected son.

To receive the Injeel from Allah

and proclaim the Lord is One.

But how would Maryam now face the people,

for this baby had no father?

A Prophet of Allah he surely was,

but would her people believe her?

In this moment, Allah consoled Maryam.

She was commanded to fast and not speak at all.

With this guidance, Maryam returned;

carrying her new-born, her miracle.

What a scene to be witnessed,

As Maryam appeared with a child.

The people were perplexed and astounded,

"Where has this baby come from?" they riled.

Maryam merely pointed to the baby,
as she had been instructed.
The people could not understand.
"Surely a baby cannot talk!" they said.

They all watched in awe
as another miracle began to unfold.
Baby Isa ﷺ turned to his people
and by the permission of Allah… he spoke!

A Prophet! A Miracle!
A sign from Allah.
What a blessing! A mercy!
To the people of al-Aqsa.

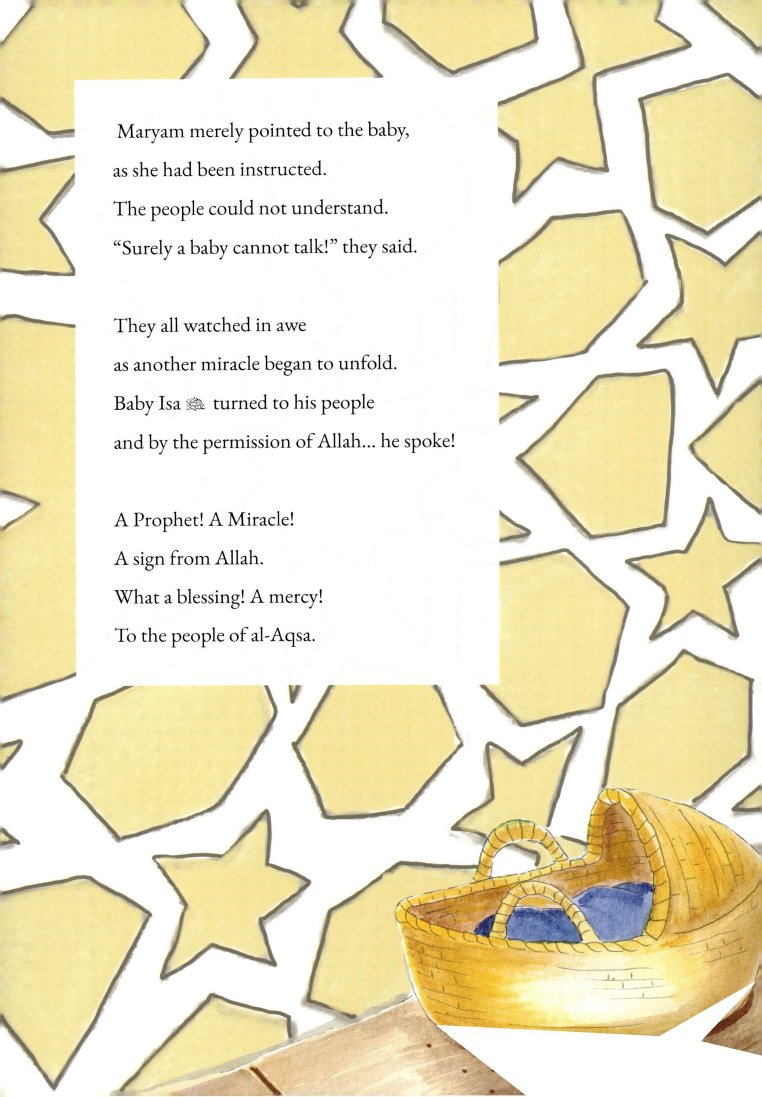

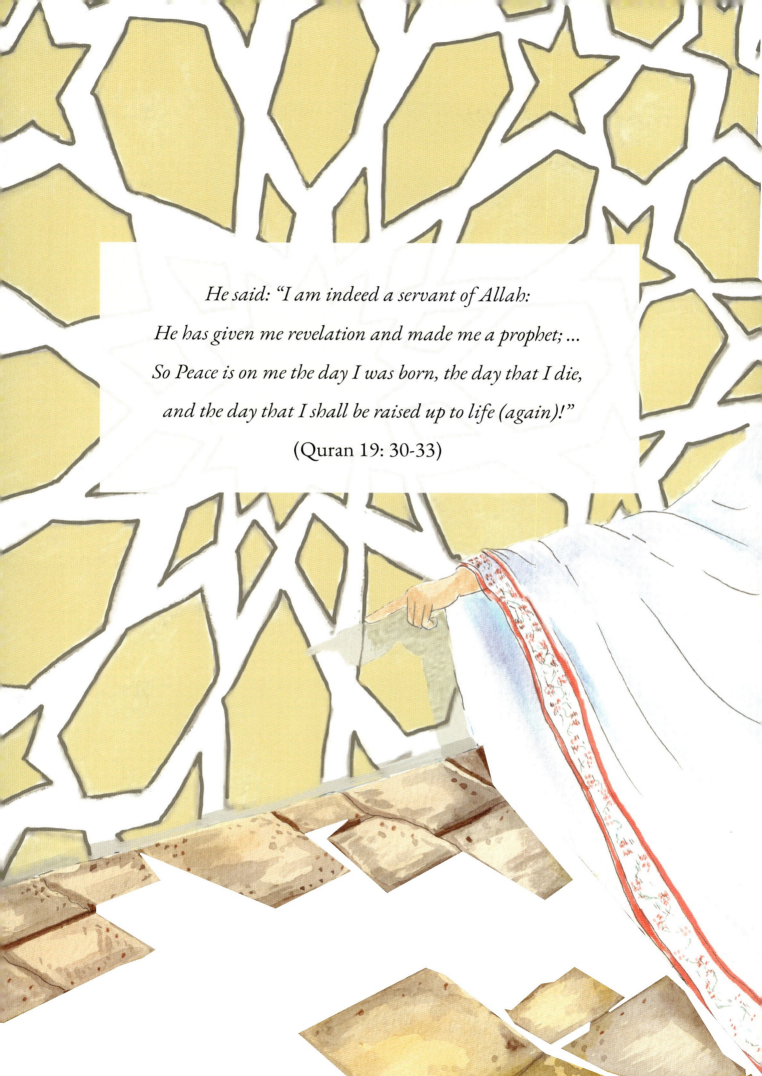

He said: "I am indeed a servant of Allah:
He has given me revelation and made me a prophet; ...
So Peace is on me the day I was born, the day that I die,
and the day that I shall be raised up to life (again)!"

(Quran 19: 30-33)

Isa ﷺ the Prophet

Now as the years were passing by,

and young Isa ﷺ was growing wiser,

he observed the world full of corruption,

for they had forgotten the teachings of Prophet Musa ﷺ.

Cheating, hatred and jealousy,

were now their common traits.

Changing the word of Allah in the Torah,

for the sake of worldly gains.

Seeing his people engulfed in sin,

Prophet Isa ﷺ was ordered to proclaim,

"I am a Messenger so follow me,

and the Mercy of Allah you will attain."

Prophet Isa ﷺ was sent with revelation,

to guide his people back to the truth.

He was a servant and a Messenger;

a link in the chain of Prophethood.

However, the Israelites mocked and scorned,

as was the way of the disobedient.

They ridiculed and opposed him,

shamelessly abusive and obstinate.

But the Prophet continued his mission
despite their attempts to stop him.
They threatened and humiliated him;
even disregarded his blessed mother, Maryam.

What indecency! What cruelty!
Isa, *alayhis salam* was gravely insulted.
They now demanded he show them miracles
to prove he was truly a prophet.

Allah, in His Infinite Mercy,
Allowed Prophet Isa ﷺ to respond to their requests.
He breathed life into a clay bird, restored the eyesight of a blind man,
cured the leper, and even brought life back to the dead.

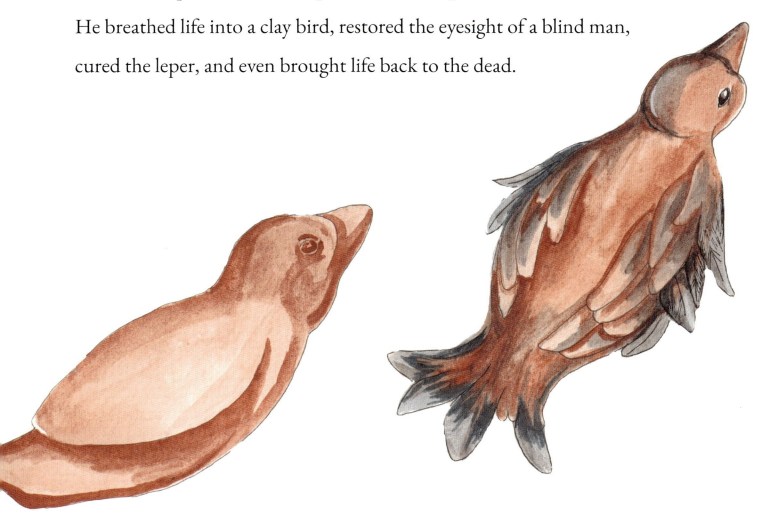

Right before their very eyes,

these miracles took place.

How could they now deny him?

His path they should surely embrace!

But to the warnings of the Prophet, they were deaf.

And to the clear signs of Allah, they were blind.

Their hard hearts were closed to the truth

and the blessings of Allah they denied.

An Evil Scheme

Nonetheless, Prophet Isa ﷺ was not dissuaded;
he called to the worship of One God.
His message was the same as previous Prophets,
and that of the Final Messenger, Muhammad ﷺ.

As the message of Isa, *alayhis salam* spread,
and the news of his Prophethood grew;
his followers stepped forward as his Disciples
proclaiming, "we believe!", though they were few.

Inspired by Prophet Isa's trust in Allah,
they asked for a feast to be sent from Heaven.
They insisted the request be made,
in order that their faith be strengthened.

So a feast Allah granted;

yet another miracle for all to see!

But as Prophet Isa's reputation spread,

the enemies grew in their animosity.

Secretly, they joined forces with the Romans

and plotted to kill the Prophet.

Too foolish they were to recognise,

that Allah is the One Who will protect.

You see, as they planned, Allah planned;

and He is the Best of Planners.

Their evil and cunning plot,

would surely be brought to tatters.

The Ascension

It was on a still Friday night

that the house of Isa ﷺ was surrounded.

Among twelve men and the Prophet;

an idea was propounded!

Isa ﷺ asked, 'Which of you will give up his life

to earn a place in Paradise?'

Bravely, the youngest of them stepped forward

and Allah placed upon him a disguise.

Unseen by all who see,

Prophet Isa ﷺ then ascended.

The villains entered to find their victim (or so it seemed);

but from their treachery he was defended.

You see, Allah made it seem as though they had killed the Prophet
by putting another in his place,
When in reality He had raised him up to the Heavens.
Prophet Isa ﷺ is surely alive and safe!

From the prayer of Maryam's mother, Hannah

and the miraculous birth of Maryam's son,

Allah's plan is always destined;

to the day we shall see Prophet Isa's return.

It will be towards the end of time

that Prophet Isa ﷺ shall descend.

He will destroy the Dajjal (the Anti-Christ),

and the true religion he will defend.

He will submit with those who submit to One God,

spreading peace and worshipping the Divine.

Finally, he will affirm he is no more than a Messenger,

just as he had been the whole time.

Such is the bounty of Allah;

The Just, the King.

The Most Gracious, the Most Powerful;

nothing can compare to Him.

For He is in no need of a son;

The Eternal, the Absolute.

He begets not, nor is He begotten,

and that, is the Ultimate Truth.

Now, this is but part of Prophet Isa's tale;

the ending is yet to be told.

His mission is not yet complete,

a story which will certainly unfold.

References

Ashraf, S. A., *The Prophets* (Ta-Ha Publishers, 1996)

At-Tahrir, H. A., *Stories of the Ambiya' for Children* (Zam Zam Publishers, 2013)

Dhorat, M. S., *Sayyiduna 'Isa A Prophet of Islam* (Islamic Dawah Academy)

Katheer, I., *Stories of the Prophets* (International Islamic Publishing House, 2006)

Khan, S., *The Greatest Stories from the Quran* (Goodwordkidz, 2001)

Nadwi, A. H. A., *Stories of the Prophets* (UK Islamic Academy, 1990)

Yusuf Ali, A., *The Holy Quran: Translation and Commentary* (Islamic Vision Ltd, 2001)

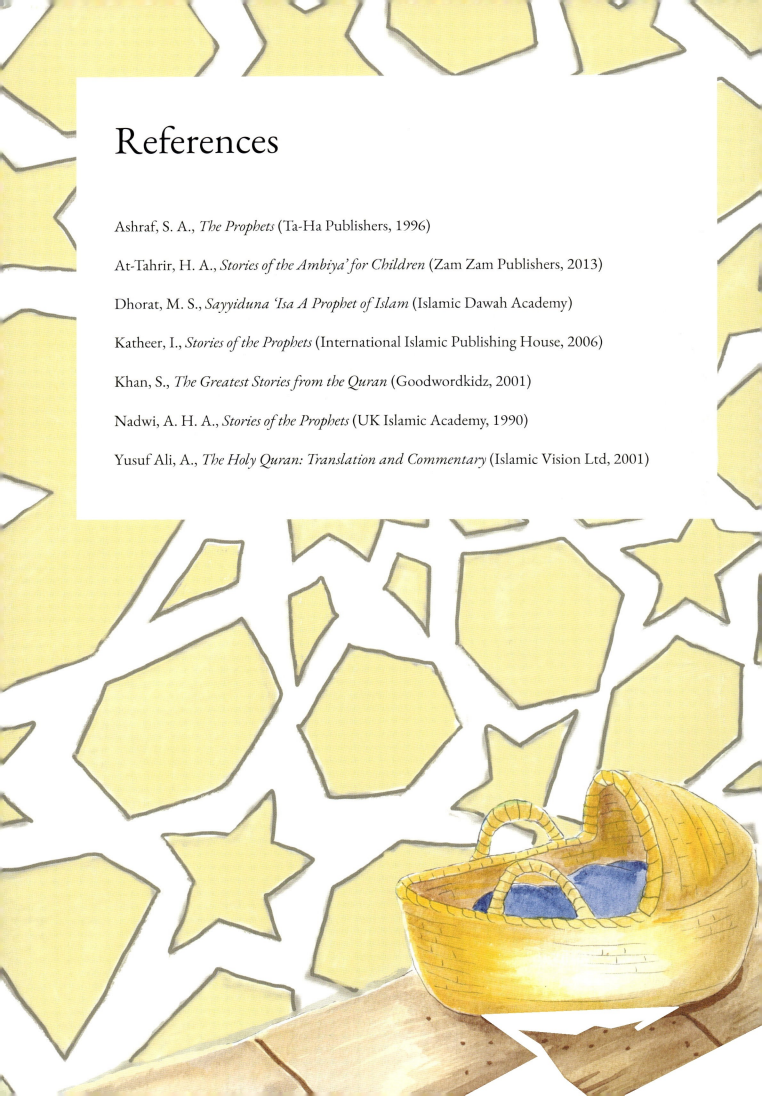